LATENESS

A BOOK OF POEMS

LATENESS:
A BOOK OF POEMS

BY DAVID SHAPIRO

The Overlook Press
Woodstock, New York

Also by David Shapiro

JANUARY

POEMS FROM DEAL

A MAN HOLDING AN ACOUSTIC PANEL

THE PAGE-TURNER

Published in 1977 by
The Overlook Press
Lewis Hollow Road
Woodstock, N.Y. 12498
ISBN: 0-87951-058-7
Library of Congress Catalog Card Number: 76-47073

To my father and in memory of my mother

Acknowledgements

The author gratefully acknowledges the following journals, in which certain of the poems in this book first appeared: *Spectator, Columbia Review, The Boston Arts Review, The Little Magazine, Times Literary Supplement, Gallery, The Connection, Poetry* (Chicago), *Partisan Review, CAPS Anthology, New Directions, Poetry Mailing List, New York Arts Journal, Nobodaddy Press, Sun, The Oxford Literary Review.*

Contents

PART I

MUSIC WRITTEN TO ORDER

Now and then, now and then, now and then
Now-ness and then-ness
And between now and then
You hear the sound of a projector
And revisit your ancient home, your new home of late.

You find only the gardener's sun has survived,
A detail that wanted to be a Psyche
Writing daily squibs to the dead.
A white breast on a white nipple would make a nice sculpture.
But you would want more milk.

You would want Mother back.
You go where you must go, Naomi goes
With Ruth, the record with the record player
Adults move magnetised to the earth.
All other insects forage at random . . .

Yes the early Christians wore masks
And had listened to Terence
Accounting for the look of no look
Cubicle said to be that of Love and Psyche

Consciousness you loved
Rounds you preferred
Sliding into the sky, looking wearily past the pink
                    toward the white
Where everything is unsigned, unsinged

In the life of the individual as well as the state
everything is late
An old vine on three stories
Of brick administration building that cannot administrate

Snow in the strictest sense
Snow so grasped I could hold to be a fiction
We profited by the wind
Twining up a rainspout, a wire, or the chain link fence

Through persian blinds again
Big emphasis on little jealousies
Taking the part for the part again
Is it rain or ripples on that stream of sphinx white paper

Inside, the unknown girl in a circle
Looks shyly down
Bone necklace and ghostly braids seeping
Into the blue air of the postcard

A day like Swiss Independence
Every door you closed I have opened
Reality more strong than the traitor's arm
Quite vanquished me

Your hands were blooded bloom
Now the tide hastes out of the view of whims
The sonatas and the caprices unaccompanied
Unaccompanied now and needing no accompaniment

The sluggish window rose
Upon a vista truly opaque:
The view golden but cold, Mother.
Cold Pastoral! Sister.

The sluggish window rose
Upon the inside-outside scene:
So the mind turned to finishing
Excited, near the truth.

With lips upon your back
The pleasure of seeing you
Replaced by the pleasure of not seeing you.
Yet you see me every moment, and momently—

When you see the oak leaf, pierced
In purple and stapled to paper
When you see the brindled grid, and now you see
The house of music splashed with ink.

CONCEALED WORDS

The parts of speech got tangled up
There need be no order and no questions
and no players guessing which quiet game is fun
no map of the world or outline of your face
as memory of you is a bad master
so it's our job to draw you like your France
or my Russia placed in truant space
in alternating colors like bones
Another game played lying down
"Wretch how could you deceive as you deceft
She answered, I promised to cleave and I've cleft"
What tree is often found in ladies' mouths?
What flower do they tread under foot?

They took me to the operating room
and took out my E—energy etc.
We thought of each other as food
Two wrongs as good as a feast
The fairest universe driven to pasture with a blow

You traded proverbs, skipped from instrument to instrument,
Musical instruments like the longest rivers
Scouting for words, for concealed words
I played with the imaginary opponent in the centre
                    of a tracery of lines of colour
Going always in the direction of arrows.

I HAVEN'T

Do you have a lion in your house?
Do you have a serpent in your house?
No fortunately I do not have a lion in my house.

Do you have a woman leaning slightly past the spirals in
    your house?
No I do not have the edge of her dress in my house.
Do you have a lion in your house?

No I do not have the outline of her body in my house.
Do you have a trouvaille in your house?
No fortunately I do not have a lion in my house.

Do you have the goddess Hygeia headless as a house?
No I do not have her right hand casting a shadow on my house.
Do you have a lion in your house?

No I do not have her light peplos folds full of life in my house.
Do you have "truth is the consequences" in your house?
No fortunately I do not have a lion in my house.

What do you have in your high heavy house?
Do you have a rendering of her brilliant pitiless hair falling
                on your house?
Do you have a lion in your house?
No fortunately I do not have a lion in my house.

RIVULET NEAR THE TRUTH

Sunken rocks are sunless
like a fence in iniquity
or a hedge in oblivion
or sunshine at supper
like the Supreme Being in surgery
restrained by oscillating powers
sweeping the dirty body
useless as if agreeable stuff
like saccharine might look upon
love's clean teeth

Sheep have no tact
at least that one can appreciate
and the playhouse is hidden
like a title on a title page
Today we lie down doing time
listening to Khachaturian's Violin Concerto
a small quantity of music
the guitar the hat the heart
up to the quick and up upon and in with
touched in the wind next to you
traces of a harness like a lattice

in the backyard in space
so we amused ourselves
under true pretences
swimming in leaves bankrupt as Danae
begging in befuddlement
meddling in water in dirty water
excited by mud
fainting with color like Davy Jones
dancing on the back step
upon nothing on war dances
St Vitus attended us
the dove splashing and then
immersed us with a blow
launched into lightness

Sophocles had not written his *Aeschyleia* yet

There are two kinds of sleep
orthodox and paradoxical
During orthodox there are no dreams
but normal diplomatic relations
like a sentence made up to include
the sleepers of the whole alphabet
all the tired out explanations
actually a hole in the ground
concealing a sniper with a sound
of spiders coasting on a rubber ocean
constantly infusing poison in the fly
with the kiss a mother reserves for
a violent child a silk of shiny metal

After an hour of that kiss
paradoxical sleep begins
and it lasts ten minutes
before orthodox is resumed

I believe that orthodox
sleep (the big changes, playing many parts,
silence dissolved by a file)
serves a function and that paradoxical
sleep (a micro-chip and micro-
instabilities) is important, too

But we are alive another way

The vista out this window makes
a plea in a vague style
pale as a persian blind
giggling like refined gold
tempted to please like a pill: Look
The loophole is opening now
looming like a looking glass
the thirsty soul examines
itself and we each other
As it is said you hug
a belief as the playhouse is hidden

PHOTO VERITABLE

Clouds cover the earth
Passengers leave but the
clouds remain. The passengers
would like to nestle and ride
in the cancerous breasts
of the sky. But the clouds
are willful and shout as
they fly: "Dirigent, dirigent
dirigent and wealthy." You will live
like a god and like it, too.

STAY STAY STAY STAY

It is snowing on the kindergarten
It is snowing on your eyelids

Love's dice
Are manias and fights
Anacreon writes
You are standing on my eyelids
And your hair
Is in my hair
As Paul Eluard
Says elsewhere
And what do you say? I say

Stay stay
stay stay
streak intrinsicality

NEEDED INVENTIONS

The problem of the firefly
Is such a delicate one
If we could only copy the firefly exactly
This problem might be done

I loved you
So I wrote on this toy blackboard
Now my crank's heart is moved
And erases every word

All airplanes, all whistles, all tunes
Operate it seems by slugs
Our train puffs and chugs
Passing through and through the loudspeaker

They're calling the names that end in y
But you fly away in airplanes
The blowtorch likes to start itself
On its own harmless 4th of July

The earth is under us
Like cheap non-fading wallpaper
The baseball bat cannot break
The violin string lasts even longer

You and I replaced by noise and wet snow
Pushed off the snowshovel onto the step
Forest fire fighters
We are alive if trapped

Now the streets are zippered up
Old teachers fold their nylon tents
Leaves burn as I pick them up
The window closes and the thief-proof fence

We wake up because someone plays viola
But in our sleep we set diamonds
So they could never work loose
And we cut time in half like stones

It was a cheap picnic
The paint brush got hard with paint
You tried to fly away on snow sleds
But the buildings interlock

Father removes the staple from his thumb
Mother looks at the clothespin
Made of wire, it is guaranteed for a life-time
You enter, with the perfection of what is not needed!

AN AFTERNOON WITH A LION

Towards the lion and up to the lion:
First you were too dazed to gaze into the lion,
Around the lion and with the lion.

Hand over hand you were getting into the lion,
Sniffing palm trees and floating upon the lion
Towards the lion and up to the lion.

In the seventh frame you slipped above the lion
Into the white sky beyond each lion,
Around the lion and with the lion.

Now under the lion, smiling under the lion
It's a light green day edges toward the lion,
Towards the lion and up to the lion.

But how is one to get out of the lion,
One's hat and stick sticking out of the lion,
Around the lion and with the lion?

You ran away from the lion and away from the lion—
Amazed and apart, days away from the lion—
Towards the lion and up to the lion,
Around the lion and with the lion.

FIELDS IN FLOOD

As the tides sweep across the surface of the earth
We a very large couple slow down on our bed
And the phonograph is rotating like the fly in the window
Squirrel walks across the park, looking for the feasible nut

And you are wrapped in a hanging mass of ropes
I a man in the distance dropping a lump of snow
A fish jumps into the arms of the carousel
We individual blurs overlap each other

I started to count you
The instant the universe came into being
Still, I am very far from having completed the job
The rain falls on the turntable, two black blobs

This is not a photograph of your face
You do not show up clearly, just lucky blood
Raindrops slowed down and or staying inside the room
Rain moving around to be followed, entering your cold body

SNOW AT NIGHT

When they took Albert Einstein home
He put on some casual clothes and took a walk
They gave him the ice-cream special
      called "The Balt"
            The violinists were leaving but not rapidly
            They remind me of time Albert said
            Always going but never gone
            But it's only eleven o'clock I said
Albert pointed to the cone thumb first, then to himself
Einstein and I nibbled our ice-cream cones
We looked out the window and said nothing
Both of us finished our cones at the same instant
            Under a lamp he gave a student his umbrella
            The snowflake kept falling on the notebook
In Los Angeles now
Einstein felt the earth shake under his foot

The second fiddler was Queen Elizabeth
Tea under the chestnuts, and a walk through the grounds
            Passing on the king's regrets for
              being away
        Adding, You came down from your peak of knowledge
        And gave me a shiny glimpse
Einstein finished his ice-cream and handed the waitress some money
The waitress gave him his change over the counter
            She thought about the tip
The ice cream and the snowflakes and the earthquakes
  It didn't work out and he didn't like it
He had put the knife in someone else's hand
It was very hard and he hated it

SCREEN

The window-shade
is a small quantity

Shades:
—of death
—of difference
—of evening

Shading
    off

into insubstantial
    copies

small
accompaniment

It is thin,
the window-shade

and thin events
come forth

May your window-shade never
    be less

your courtesy

and your shadowy

deep

frame

PART II

THE DEVIL'S TRILL SONATA

I

As Aeschylus puts it
in Frag. 351: Let us say what comes to our lips, whatever it
may be; or perhaps, Let's say what's on
the tip of our tongue.
    As Achilles put it to Apollo,
You have made a fool of me.

It was with some interest
I noticed the violin back in its case
of itself, was playing the piece
correctly and with almost
no trepidation of the string!
It played along and is playing
by and of and for itself—

And that was the end of our friend
The wisest and best on this earth lightly inclined—
"Be mute for me,
contemplative violin."

You clamp the rifle and release the bullet
And you know that it will always reach the target
And the ferryboat sails straight across the river:
It feels normal in the still air.

What course must the aviator set
On a level road when the day is wet?
The tracks of the raindrops on the window
Are dropped from the bridge by a boy.

You place a smooth box down like a stone
And you rest on your own inclined plane.
A stone is seen to pass through the window
But now the stone is snow.

We have so few red flowers
The stem hangs over the edge of the table
The flower leaves the stem like an aviator
Or like the man in the elevator.

The milkweed fills the sky
Which is small, pale blue, and almost white
Like the game lit up at night.
"We have reached the bottom, you and I."

Half-divine, half-raw, half-German, half-Greek
Time now for an excursus to the centre of all this muddy junk
I gaze into the hilarious sky where flowers gather unknowingly
The last row in a theatre of stars

Dear cloud, free from moral guilt
I see you dragged like a heap of small sacrificial cakes or
                              swerve
Streets tarry in one place, and satirical teeth bite and corrode
Stinging clouds are worse

Oh clouds I fall fighting against the whole Persian army
A pond's another place where streetlights delight to roll
                              in gewgaws and larvae
Andromeda, make steady my steps
You who had but lately begun to exist, who existed formerly

The sun is hot and scalds the little day.
The plane sails up, stalls slightly, drops its nose in a dive
Into a barrel of dimes.
What tree always has a partner?

. What flower do most people go far to avoid?
You are beginning to find a bed very boring
Yet you are not allowed to sit up more than an hour at a time.
Mother stands straight up at Green's Five and Ten Cent store.

A supply of white floating soap, and you are all ready to carve up
This tray holds all I need;
It's a nice clean occupation.
But I am not sure what these incalculable beasts may do.

You need a ticket of admission to my rooms.
Naomi and I make up contrite items and float them down the stairs.
You are lying on your back in the honeysuckles—choking.
My entire life was being decided by five nincompoops.

Father says, I will get you a glass of water
If you will bring me a leaf from the linden.
So you ran to the linden tree, crying Dear linden, dear linden,
Give me one of your leaves.

We must keep this heat.
That is. we let our clothes get cold instead of ourselves.
Three shirts are warmer than the whole out-of-doors
And the soft inside part of the house. Because we are
                half air ourselves.

What is the difference between a cloud and a spanked boy?
Dear Sky, we who are about to slide (on ice) salute you.
I take my snowy map and look at one country for three minutes
Only a minute to go; that's not asking much of your memory.

Up goes the curtain; Columbus discovers America.
In this story your hands play the part of empty barns.
Up goes the curtain; Cornwallis surrenders at Yorktown.
You open your hand to show the five sheep sleeping safely
          under the tree, which ladies wear around
          their neck.

The horizon is an accumulation of dissolved sky materials
And the sky is an illustration: for example, you appear
As a diagram would make you clear or attractive.
A cloud leaps from one place to another, wishing ill to enter.

One horizon is strikingly like a shady tree,
But inferior and has no sweet or edible fruit
          for the mind's imago.
All insects are illiterate, and your mistake also
Is marked by the immeasurable crudity of your shroud of a
          parachute.

As you begin to shred it, the lateral support from the clouds
Lifts and contracts your shoulders, and you fall
Through an indifferent or averse heaven to end covered with shrubs
Resembling a shrub actually, and shucking off your little
          wrinkled skirt in the sword grass.

This picture of you consists predominantly of wingless insects
Hurtling through the air on superficial wounds,
Finally adhering to certain showily blotched flowers
Where the gradient was so gentle the blue current was invisible.

The gradient is so gentle the current is invisible.
If twilight is a state of imperfect clarity
Then this is a period in decline. Like the bare leg of
            a cautious business man on a polar night
Regarded as a kind of gratuitous addition.

There we are, like two crystals grown together
In a specific rational manner, twin city in full night
With set arias and binoculars adapted for use at the opera,
And you so silky stretched over and under me like a steel frame.

In the dim light, a romantic mollusk closes his shells
And the bodily process suggests a lid. Ophelia green
            like so many mottled rocks
Drifts with her kin in an area without trees:
Two pages face one another in a book.

Mouth widely open,
The heart-shaped heart, strung typically with one string,
And now scattered under mature trees in sheet from pig iron
In a planned series of moves as at the beginning of the world.

Book with no cover or with a flush paper cover
Urging us to do something and attacking one's past
Rotating the television camera like the Greek god of the forests:
You alone lack the implication of any previous activity or
            agitation.

You are calm in the following strife and archaic heat
And the children stay behind with a little French.
The fool had to be tricked to finish her dinner by then,
But we two cherished our certain defeat. The rain shot down
            in an especially casual manner.

And the snow began to plink at random targets,
As if the earth were a plotting board,
And moving like someone dropping in water, you fell
Under the dim umbrella's stained umber.

In the clear and putrid water, like a necklace of gobs
Floating and dividing, dividing and growing, clinging,
The basis of your earth is wet and clings to the wet:
Muddy valves, in air and trees, muddy food.

The reindeer walk by the running water.
All week we were attracted to some point.
Like animals that are food for human beings, world-wide lichen
              and air on occasion filled with balls and
              sexual spores
You brought yourself into water, into darkness, into quiet water.

In July we broke like strings, swimming in sea lettuce.
And now like specimens too old to be allowed to dry
Before mounting, merely floated onto the business paper
To which we will finally fasten ourselves and adhere,
              under pressure

Like brown shoelaces, growing in bed or in the garden
Common as stones and shells, held erect by the air
And reaching you by summer and there rot, not easily seen.
When you died, a harmless bird was permitted to
              disappear from our sky.

Little is known, but spiders are found in birds' stomachs
And rats have taken to living in trees, in mongoose country;
Jacob sent pistachio nuts into Egypt; a hot summer day;
You see my white shadow on the wall, it's Caspar the
      friendly Ghost.

Never again to trust the sea for delicate spots
And so we sink, diving and dabbling where you go
And doctors float by on hands in the burnt umber sands
And you faint murmuring of the terrible somersaults of shells.

Bad likeness. We climbed to the highest available point
With your perfume of sick whales
With your ninety foot wives and their eighty-nine foot guys
All opening their mouths, slothfully clinging to twig and leaves.

Twigs as well as leaves we were tolerant of each other.
Suddenly the heal-all had a height of two feet
Many found themselves stuck in duplication of time
As well as instants of music, simple flower.

"Thimble flower" and you too smooth and finely fuzzy.
In the night kidney-shaped and grey
The telephone crowds massed through the turnstile
On way to the voting machine:

Infamy lay on your lips and nightly teeth
Your hands pointed out the seven seas
Dusk opening and remaining open until morning
Branched and unbranched and had its poisonous effects.

Pilots file by, in air, but the mountain is shrewd and
     circumvents them.
In the dim Italian operation room
As the doctors dance this dialogue is spoken: Gastrula,
     bastula,
This music is continuous, as you intertwist and vessels
     are cut in two by sailors, doctors.

One relates to this to the point of frenzy, which it hates.
The children stay on their seesaws, in underwear and their
     outer clothing.
But the ground is slowly oozing out of the park
As Mae West was noted for herself and inflatable life jackets.

     In the earth departed souls slide by
     In a world of organised crime below the level of ordinary
          life
Their colors seen through waves and forfeited land,
Beach that failed to appreciate the risks involved.

With a message in code: Returning from abroad.
The harvest is soft, the beach white, and your breath is assent.
Wiser the nobody, the father to the thought,
The wind deviating as a bee joins a few excluded plants.

I should eagerly like to know anything.
To limit my statement to an ascending climax
Let you take advantage of this googol of forget-me-nots
Like that big blue bumblebee drawing himself up for a speech:

Come unto me all ye who labor and are heavy laden
To prepare for the Flower-Exam, and failing
              twice, become a whole ghost of pollen
To be on the way in the wind
The skin all dressed up, apples brewing, odors
              looming, and events winding into fermentation.

Next you write the girl's name, fold over,
              and pass along.
Then the sentence where we met, prepared for whatever
              might happen like the pavement.
Next what you did; what I did; what you said;
What I said; the consequence; what the world said.

I said, Do give me a kiss, whatever may happen.
You dusted off my coat. I hit you with a million dollars
              worth of mislaid gold.
So you decided to dive into these weeping clouds,
              tackling them without difficulty.
The world said, "That's what they said."

Amusing resident of rooms in which we live,
I remember you when every tree was filled with you.
Now the fool is parted from his lasso
Harmless pleasures a thimbleful of fluid might erase.

Tooting in the miasma, along the serrated edges.
You lie in wait, in the throat of the flower.
The slow ones and I stay behind, obeying death.
The slower ones stay on a single flower.

A painful shadow settles on the second violin.
Your hiding places are limited and easily localised.
In the back seat, sprinkled with introductions, we kissed
A sparrow then I built in trash

Because of your delicate nature I stuck to paper
As the heavenly eye closes, the lion reaches climax
The spider jumps and hides in silky nests
Now disentangled we abscind in snips and fritter away our trips

A woman showed her nipples on TV
And inserted a syringe injecting milk
Into her slightly swinging breasts.
And a lovelier woman bent her head to suck.

The shirt of Dejanira flaps in the air, streaming.
And you stretched out on the bed, enigma and reward.
Or we who embraced flap loose from head to foot.
You have done nothing but try to stand on your hands
                    for ten seconds

To win the one way out of a sad course.
But it is not nothing: the tuneful music, little elegant doubts.
Tabula rasa is no joke.
They killed Niobe. Cartaga delenda est.

Oh bees one pound of your honey represents twenty thousand trips
Each trip a mile, and every individual must die
The fragrant flowers shudder when you give your extreme sting
But these plants are not easily affected by our thoughts

My thoughts easily affected by the frosts and draughts
Thoughts in the muggy swamp air flash
"Like a match held near this orange flower
When the snowflake falls on the toothache tree"

Angelica is stripped to her smooth bare skin a common complaint
Fortunate to wake with her question seeming part of it all
What is the difference between sterile and fecund?
What is a dome? What does Chant d'amour mean?

We would sail away in this big conversation
Take it in our heads to go into the financial purse together
Find only empty islands so our tears would patter on rivers
            like tins of kerosene
And when I saw you I would gobble up rivers, matchboxes and all.

When you are asleep I will appear and do that some more
And pass the winter like Caesar in Gaul
So I race after you but you put up the storm windows
I lie in bed like the happy book in the library,
            in spite of poverty and pain.

And one day a dry wind blows fractions of a postcard at my feet
The wind that likes to whisk you out of bed
And cover all the space it can reach, swerving
Carefully away, into the black like the balls in the tennis court.

There was no lead in the lead pencil.
There is no bone in whalebone.
In bed your tissue-balloons exploded and Louisa May Alcott
            and the long-hoarded dimes
And you came to give orders to your devoted subjects,
            who shivered into pieces.

This was our game for the old pack of opponents
And it could be played flat on your back.
You twirled the old cards and aimed right for my head
You advised me to draw the lines lightly, so they could be
easily erased.

Now I see your pictures of a goose presence and rabbit identity.
Each of those creatures must be and is threatened with
insanity.
Dropping to your knees, you protected my old mirror
from the lunging air
In it, your own face was white, like candles on the Christmas tree.

When we were tired out we fell among fishermen
You and I swore on sunny seaweed that this penny would be
eternally hidden under the rocks
You enjoyed the quietness of the raindrops falling into pans.
Each drop has vengeance in it. We sat all night
speculating on the baleful spray.

We floated on the big bed like crystal madness.
You liked the flights of those lost pencils all right
Now we will overlap like the ancients with their chains
Shaking them each day, as they are tightened more strongly.

And the fountain ran on, step by step freely falling
And we loved the swath of the evening
You against the balustrade of detested tin
And I leaned against the riddled curtain of your breast.

You hid beneath the grillework roses with a hundred fears.
You suggested to your little patient that I judge the
            height of these roses.
You tore and tore and buried your teeth in me, but
            I couldn't let go.
Under the rainy rainbow we would lie and struggle like sparks.

Wild coca-cola is easy to find
My own humble lot resembles that of a broken pill
To which I've soared on wings of song
Floating into the land of mystical peaches

My architecture aged one being ruined
Like so much ordinary rice, white! China's greatest architect!
That repeating erector rubber band rifle
Nearly blinded my best friend from the top of the stairs

Botanists behave idiosyncratically outside the Park
The furry elm-tree has moved further away
But when the tiny dragonfly attempts the Atlantic Ocean
Who will be able to force it from that far?

Hand in hand we fled the plain-clothes policeman
What good do parents by smiting their drums
Through thousands of miles of white papers
I direct my happy gaze to the television. A quarter of a
            century ago you were one

Like ordinary white rice, rice! China's youngest poet!
And we filled up their bed, Judy, Naomi, and I
And you had to pull it out of closets and look down
            the dumbwaiter corridor
Your face wet with ink

Medea found Jason;
Penthisilea stunned Achilles;
Omphale held Hercules, and Semiramis led a whole country.
Two boys lie under the Empire State Building, naked and crushed.

Only the day is a surprise; the clouds consist entirely
            of ice-crystals.
Why should the old bride keep her distance?
Only the day is a surprise.
As they plunge through her she is heated by friction
            to incandescence

And they leave the old bride in luminous streaks
Before she disintegrates completely,
Falls back into bed with the explosive force of a meteorite.
I approach your metal mouth, you put it near me.

Oh silk that supports the world
That shakes the delicate sun and seals light in paper bags
Brushed up or burnt up or wandering or trapped
The tree is girdled round by disintegrating bark. The pencil
            sharpener filled with a heavy object with a
            need to be turned.

In the other world, in the beginning of polychrome
By the sun's lid, the mule goes down to the ocean
            and the girl throws away her shoes
In your own boat you wait to ferry across some dead young woman,
Who has no boat.

I heard you were draughting pyramids
In the land of wild coca-cola
The days of our days together are filled with sour plums
This whole muddy May has ruined my white suit

It's as if we were at the fingerboard, the keyboard together
And my throat were being torn by a crying gibbon
Whose voice could be heard throughout Washington
Crying, Liar! liar! I have something to say to you all!
          Come to the eastern mirage-tower at once!

Next week I shall sail down on toy boats with physicists
Going as far as physicists can go, looking for you
The thought one couldn't buy you has shattered this
          homemade mirror moon
That is the white suit, which has flown into the sky

Your heart-shaped boat was dragged through the air
Your stream-lined body moved into the stream
In this room, you are only a drop of blood, Science says
And you have just completed your tour of my heart

There are worlds above us, too;
The inhabitants of Jupiter don't use psychoanalysis,
          which they call The Shadows.
Those of Mercury object to the expression of ideas by voice.
Too material, and they have a language of the eye;

Saturnians are tormented by depression.
Moon people, small as four year olds, speak from the stomach
        and crawl around;
Venusians are gigantic but gaga and live by robbery.
Part of Venus, however, is inhabited

By beings of great gentleness, like you and me
Who live, loving, wrong to set foot on the earth.
Part of Venus, however, is inhabited
By those with remarkable red lips and brown eyebrows and
        the diaphanous joints of a crab:

Light brown at the heart, shaded to green,
        and cut into many delicate teeth.
There is intelligence in paradise. Musicians practise
        in sublimity. Only in the music is there
        the slightest crisis.
The leg worships neutrally. The eye signals from a height,
        and the hip moves locked like a dove.

The boar that killed Adonis
Snuffled around the bushes in the backyard.
While two celli played their parts in the trio, a house
        was raised in accompaniment on concrete pilotis:
Inside, music, and outside "frozen music."

She had reduced her methodology to zero.
The ferry-colored stars—stars the color of the Staten
        Island Ferry—
Were strong defiant instruments in glass
Rather like sunlight in a cup.

Swarming with opaque veins into its chair, and clucking,
The air mail envelope hid in a cloud.
You feel that you belong to an era of evergreen trees and
                flying reptiles, not this one
Strapped to the deep-rooted and luminous Dog Star.

You had taken a small sip of a continuous flow
Like a hobby a child pretends to hide
Locking doors and resting after a squabble seemed to sever forever
Relations, as a ship suspected of carrying disease
                is forbidden the shore.

II

Lightly you touch me
paper on which I write
Problems have turned into snow at night
like a little car abandoned in the midst of vague terror

The Bobbsey Twins departed for the depot
Ready for Marat and just as ready for Tiberius
What was the purpose of this journey to Moscow?
I do not think it was clear to themselves

I am closest to you, Earth
and you a pale steel-blue
Life captive in snowbanks
protecting a mouse from a hawk

Like a sex organ on a bright green mat
you favored the cool streams
but you were merely a moss.
Our house a bulky mass of grass, feathers and trash,
        tucked into a high rise

Under a quarrelsome tree of blue sky
We were flying seventeen miles an hour among the poplars
Phyllis is dead and we keep hearing summer songs
while others are prostrate in weeds in snow.

This moment is gone forever
Like a snowflake on a river
And for emergency mattresses
Man uses Spanish moss

Adults move in zigzags
Not necessarily toward the North
Into darkness or running water
Into quiet water

It should not be completely destroyed
Nor unduly encouraged
Look how the bluejay
Has taken things left idly about!

That night the oak tree was rather blunt
Not a fast grower
It had lived six hundred years
Winky the Dog was snarling back at David

The river with its fine hair
Poured out along that smooth night
"Kettle boats" were borne away in clusters
And women hung from the middle like clever pollinations

And we were seeking
Like honeybees behind the Persian blinds
As the SS Xerxes was interrupted on its green street
Your skin flushed, but I was harmless

We called each other names
like mania, convulsion, loss of sight
We became crazy eating your throat
To bring you to a specified state by sobbing
        I ordered you to judge me fairly

I liked the Runaway Star
The Giant Dumbbell Nebula, Triangulum
The Beehive and Lyra the Lyre
Like a violin in blue white fire.

You have not touched me,
but the injury is as great.
It may be we do not have enough October, November, December.
There is another approach:

Kissed in daringness.
Looked for nearby sea.
Yet to pass beneath these misted trees seems not enough.
Laughing at death as you forget the dream.

III

The earth is another appleseed
And you a poppy seed in the parking lot,
        half a mile away
We shrink away from the sun like snow
Setting up the dead men of the day before
        on stakes to terrify the enemy

You dreamt of playing Hamlet our proxy wooer
And ended up instead as Prologue to Troilus and Cressida
Whose love proved stronger than Neptune
Neptune, a pea about a mile away

We went hoping to have all thoughts
Passing through like Christmas boxes
Your own gifts moved ahead
Your brain like a tennis ball somewhere in the stands

You couldn't have had time to talk of the same river
        even once
The football flowed into the centre of the field
But some instant must have been chosen
And we moved along the path dazzled by ice on mica

What was your reaction to your brain on this street
Scratched into the distance you relied only on your knowledge
You thought up a simple reason why we must be correct
Then, like a rocket you looked up

Ophelia preferred to be silk
Rather than inside the glass
The first car hits the second, the second the third,
          and so on
Each whirlpool produces a dimple for Hamlet

Ophelia is some sort of fluid
The silk cloth is rubbed and she flows
Her comparatively small body wades into the stream
She has been rubbed off and migrates into the silk

You make a rough sketch of the swordplay
And the sword tilts
Hamlet drifts like water through the pipes
The earth is a magnet that can be switched on or off,
          but where is that switch?

We can imagine a film run backwards
Pure milk leaps into the jug
The ashes form a new log
The omelet reconverts into the chicken

The wind which reduces the snowy comedienne
          to a hat
But the hat flies back to the store
The ancient city is frost
And rubble rebuilds in a show of heat

The film didn't deceive you for too long
You saw the joke reforming
On the face of the custard pie
I am of no further use to you

You have used up all available tides by the moon on oceans
Combining in an orchestrated dissatisfaction
Eventually the day is a month
The balloon's buoyant joke is punctured and snow fills
                the whole room with disordered clothes

Lumps of clay collide
And the photograph of Ophelia trails a small bubble
Ophelia still unspent at the end of time
The fountain spouts downward

It was that small fictional dog
That eventually brought us down into the sand
There is only one real Hamlet, but the student
                is advised not to adopt it
Ophelia, there is only one true Ophelia

She hangs from her string
And the pilot cuts it
I hold you between clenched teeth like a trapeze
On the chair in which you were vainly swinging

We had no way of knowing what the insect was knowing
No "love" or "desire" of that mother bird feeding
The worm as it consciously decided to crawl away
We were so close together we gave a single impression
                on the photographic plate

Your bundle of human hairs exposed to the atmosphere
The tuning fork kept vibrating
Organ pipes and trumpets were meeting halfway
And blue-green life took place in some of the clouds

An insect walks by along the wooden rule
He is hit head-on by a puff of wind
He is wobbling slightly on the desk
        a jerk with innumerable legs
The car travels straight across the highway laughing

We fight but with violin bows
You tickle me into Fiddle Faddle on stage
July Fourth is mounted on the Deal Casino
Your sparkler reaches my heart and travels in a
        fiery path upwards

I was only your boy
On this poor but reputable stone staircase
Again you had a brown thorn in your hand
And once more you asked my help in removing it

The Day star lived on like an epileptic
Think of poor Hermia encountering Lysander
And then all the young people united in proper pairs
I went home and tumbled in vain through the dictionary

Mozart was a boy and the sonata was normal
There are no rules
But there are many songs
Easily heard by putting your ear to the window

Think of the stone staircase at Cnossos
The treads were 18 inches
And the risers 5 and a half inches
Now think of the flight which stood in front of Le Puy

The stairs still exist, nor have they yet been buried
Successive stages of a Ziggurat
Leading to another Propylaea
Or sloping corridors of the tireless Sphinx

Elsewhere, in the Chateau of Chambord
Or in the circular tower of Amboise
Or for instance the fallen one of Mark
Stairways of Ireland, wholly embedded in the earth

I a robot and you a robot-ess
Exhibiting all of the symptoms of love
As if a threshing machine
Had come to a farm

I played for you on my resonant box of peculiar strings
four open notes
in the normal pitch
Judy was picking up garbage with a bright green stick

It is a false etymology that has embedded you
in the language and now a false entry to try
                and change you
You began with your desultory raids
A trained soldier is often afraid at sea

You took two music stands and placed two equally distant
                and let a third be farther removed
In a shower of warm music
Your body in the air mail envelope revolved
Chilly in the jet's kidnapped chambers

Kinderszenen
It is a murky firmament in which to shine
This is you, wind
This is your life pushing against unbreakable panes

You were bigger than me
But you were still in the family
As a viola is in the violin family
If pitched a fifth below and empurpled

Summer dusted with pollen
Drew back
And then it pressed up like lips
As we entered the stigmatised cellars

And as we entered the Bogey Man
Edged forward with underwater spearguns
And so the sweet green violet
Was permanently closed

We were natives of Alps
And had the power of reducing all cancerous
                growth
I played you my resonant box of peculiar strings
four open notes.

Unknown woman, unknown physician, unknown Roman
Cut in two by spring vacation
Unknown man, so-called, beside me is a tiny coupon
Eaton's Berkshire Typewriter Paper A 201 and liquid
                eraser fluid:

Shake well, touch on
Blow for instant dry
Retype. Product penetrates.
The rose of the poet and the rose of the botanist are one!

But the specific achievement of America
Expressed in the scar above the temple
In which the bullet is painted, in blonde hair,
Is the unsparing "trans-naturalism," blending both head and bullet

Throwing off rain and snow like a feather
In the attic the child confronts his cardboard toys
            and waves them aside
Reduced to a few projecting ledges
On which my puppet Marcus Aurelius is perched

We note a pure distaste for growing outlines
And underneath the eraser fluid, set off
            against the high lights
And the whole surface thus scotch-taped
A compromise between a bird's eye and a continuous style,
            which cannot be successful

Time for a second coat, where the white ink smeared
Non-toxic and nonflammable
The squat figures of Senators groping for work
An open situation is what the rose prefers

A baby held on to a car
I said, Little baby, do you know where you are
One moment in Italy, the next moment in Greece
I dragged the baby through the window-seats

We passed that store of tiny books
Nancy and Sluggo walked past the park
Their father had antlers, their mother had lamps
And other living room objects on their inky heads

And children passed their calm relations
Calmly dead upon the shore
Shadowed by the rusty bulwark
And women were suddenly bitten in Florence by their dogs

The deluxe circles are empty
On infinitesimal feuilletons
Collaborations between Nancy and Sluggo
End in the living-room, when father puts out the lamps

Several falls of snow, and some sledding
True winter since the seventeenth and hard ice
We have come a long way it is good to be sleeping
Far from our starting point, your voice

Sleep pays, and time is the explanation of a brute
About a bewildering amount of red-eyed space
You I resisted but the poppies provoked me to it
The recovering breath of your sleep-drowned face

A person of doubtful meaning stabs you with a knife
All a-tremble as if circling for a fish
And you are running away precipitately with your life
Wearing the garbs of chivalry, as we kiss.

The dead play the piano.
Without instruments, but not without sounds!
Some prefer *Kinderszenen*.
We are alive, as a maple-leaf!

You notice I don't talk about Pythagoras
I don't even know if there was such a man
If you want to know what's around you
You don't look up a catalogue of appearances

I don't know how much we owe to
Pythagoreans what we call Pythagorean thought
These principles are limits, almost standards
This strained Plato and is lurking in him

Whether it's participation as Plato said
Or imitation as the Pythagoreans said
Plato grew more and more Pythagorean
He met Pythagoras in Southern Sicily

Plato announced a public lecture on the good
According to Aristotle all the people came
Wondering what Plato would say or hide
The lecture contained nothing but numbers

I walk on the dubious roof my father built
Straining to inspect the cracks that will come in my day.
The dog is an honest animal, plain-speaking as fabled
But the pelican eats him anyway, for all of his venom.

This ladder is too short, and does not reach the floor.
Nor will I descend it, though Dad request
Mother is sleepy, unhappy with all these brats
Without whom she is the happy accompanist,
        when the sonata starts

The elevator slips so far, so fast
Surely the ladder then is an improvement
On the elevator in this respect. And don't forget the
        fireman's pole
Or Rapunzel, whose hair was a staircase.

It's nice to have a kaleidoscope in the house.
You stamp your foot in the lagoon, you can't even cross
        the same river once.
Wading placidly and alive, you enjoy your borrowed toys.
You walk out for the Sunday Times and forget to return.

The sun rises above the pitcher's mound, like a mail boat
The stars are now thoroughly scotch-taped
        along the sky
And we lie together like tree-lined streets
The speed-limit sign and the white Volkswagen

The Divine Comedy of a postcard
Living on the earth is like dinner on the ground
The air is filled with warm air and torn pocketbooks
THE President has some other good news:

The sky is blank because it's blue
The sky is blank and it is blue, filled with habits,
          filled with habitable houses
Filled with spirits
"But I don't see anything"

It's a bright day in the mail boat
The sun keeps rising out of the mist, large
          and calm
The wind passes the pump house
As if it entertained great scorn of Hell

1973-1974

LATENESS

The nerves are foolish invisibility induces offers
Tears streaming as if attached to some creed
Are mildly antiseptic due to salt content
Tears secret and stainless
Precursors for the sound of your voice

People burst open and are released and release
      themselves
Easily picked up in that wind
At the lower and rounded end of the "heart"
No man ever saw those forests of fern but I see you
      in your bed
As you floundered in a stream of air and light

Blue and brown and black and hazel
The eye divested of tears like insignias with a blow
The lachrymal apparatus remains and the bright room
We are separate now and move rapidly like tears
The legs from the knees are missing

And the arms are joined awkwardly to the body
A lion tears your hair fallen low at the back
The whole world would have been the pediment
The lion's mane has successive rows of flames
In your missing hand you would have held the lion

My face, the "epigram" is carved in large red letters
Above are holes
Feet of the deceased
And traces are preserved of the wise and excellent
      doctor Aeneas
Doubt is represented and traces of blue wine with
      nine carved petals

Leaves are falling in schematic folds
The tongue of a conquered hero protrudes slightly
The face is long with a battered surface
Inscriptions we engraved on our thighs
A leaf falls from your lips and I am in love with
    my lot

Only the upper world is intoxicated
Colour would have covered you
The scene itself comes from some original
The child extends his hand in an eager manner toward
    his mother
In his hand a puppet doll of the deceased

In the hole in her right breast
Would be wedged the spear of the victorious warrior
Only her head is preserved
It turns back in agony
Thus drowns back into the depth of the shrine

It is the work of a good sculptor
It is difficult to distinguish between the living
    and the dead
The deceased plays the piano
In the airy plains of the ocean, a rich throne
    which shows
The need to heroise this woman, unjustly dead

Eros touches her lightly
With the palm of his left hand
The little refugee can scarcely stand on his feet
A young woman is leaning on her arm which, stretched
    vertically,
Closes the composition